Simple Soups

SIMPLYCANNING.COM

Simple Soups

From Canning Jars to the Soup Pot

Sharon Peterson

Home Canned Goodness
It's all in Your Hands
Doesn't it feel good!

www.simplycanning.com

Peterson, Sharon
    Simple Soups

ISBN 978-1478281849

Disclaimer and Reader Agreement

Table of Contents:

NOTE FROM SHARON:

Home preserving is part of a wonderful healthy lifestyle.
These recipes are not fancy. Simply delicious and simple to
prepare, that is what you will find here.

This delicious collection of recipes is soups made using
home canned and dehydrated goods. Preserve foods by
canning or dehydrating... and then learn to cook with it!

They are not recipes tested for processing and canning
themselves. There is a distinction there. I have not used
these recipes to preserve them.

If you want to can soups for storage on your shelf, I've
included directions on **how to adapt your recipes for home
canning.**

Stock or broth is a
main ingredient in
most of my soups. If
you have not tried to
**made your own
stock**..... you don't
know what you are
missing!

TIPS FOR COOKING WITH HOME PRESERVED FOODS.

To adapt any recipe to using home canned foods simply use an equivalent amount of the same types of food. If a recipe calls for diced tomatoes.... use home canned tomatoes. How easy is that! The flavors won't be exactly the same (often better!) This will give you a place to start developing your own favorites.

Home canned chicken or beef stock has much less salt content than a commercially produced stock or broth. Be sure to consider the salt content of the soup if you need to use commercially processed broth or bouillon. You may need to use less salt than my recipes call for.

Sometimes making a creamed soup requires using a blender to cream some of the ingredients. Avoid burns when you are blending hot liquids! Let the ingredients cool a bit first. If you are using a blender, lay a dishtowel over the lid of the blender. If any hot soup spurts out from under the lid, the towel will protect your hands and arms.

I use venison and elk for many of these recipes. If your recipe calls for browned venison stew meat, using a pressure cooker to prepare the meat ahead of time makes the meat tender and tasty.

Cube meat and sear in oil in your pressure cooker. Cover and cook at 10 pounds pressure for 10 minutes. Release pressure by running cold water over your cooker. Continue with recipe. If you don't have access to wild meat substitute with beef, no problem.

Cooking Measures and Equivalents			
4 quarts	8 pints	16 cups	128 fl oz
2 quarts	4 pints	8 cups	64 fl oz
1 quarts	2 pints	4 cups	32 fl oz
½ quart	1 pint	2 cups	16 fl oz
¼ quart	½ pint	1 cups	8 fl oz

SAFETY PRECAUTIONS

When cooking with home canned low acid foods I suggest that you boil them for 10 minutes before serving. This includes all vegetables and meats.

Low acid is any meat or vegetable. Be sure to consider this precaution if adapting your own recipe.

The recipes in Simple Soups are all boiled for more than 10 minutes in the preparations so nothing extra is needed.

There is some debate about whether this is a necessary step. Even among extension services you may get different responses. One of the most logical reasons I've read as to why this may NOT be needed is the fact that after pressure canning at high temperatures simply boiling it later is not doing much. However I've done this for so long I'm more comfortable boiling before serving.

If you have questions about the importance of boiling your low acids, call your local Agriculture Extension Service and ask for more details.

After talking with my local extension service I have decided that the extra step is not that much work and it gives me peace of mind and so I do it. I'd recommend the same for you. You'll have to decide. Boil for 10 minutes, plus one minute per 1,000 feet above sea level.

Remember these recipes are prepared with this precaution in mind so no extra boiling is needed.

Soup Recipes

Soup Recipes made with home canned and home dehydrated foods.

BEEF BARLEY SOUP

An easy inexpensive soup. Make enough to save some for leftovers. It thickens up so much on day two, call it a stew!

Ingredients:

- 1 pound lean stew beef, cut in 1/2-inch cubes
- 1/2 cup chopped onion
- 2 ribs celery, chopped
- 2 medium carrots, diced
- 3/4 cup barley
- 1 bay leaf
- 6 cups beef broth
- 2 teaspoons salt, or to taste
- pepper, to taste

Preparation: Brown stew meat in a heavy skillet.

In a large crockpot, combine stew beef with onion, celery, carrots, barley, bay leaf. If you are using home canned beef broth bring it to a boil for 10 minutes and then add to the rest of your ingredients in your crock pot. If you are using commercially prepared beef broth simply add to the crock.

Cook beef and barley soup on LOW in crockpot for 6 to 8 hours. Check and add water if needed. Your barley will swell and thicken the more it cooks.

Add more salt and pepper, to taste.

Notes: Make this with venison or elk meat as well. Using your pressure cooker to prepare the meat ahead of time makes it tender and tasty. See Tips and Hints at the front of this book for directions on how to pressure cook stew meat.

CREAMY TOMATO SOUP

You'll love this creamy tomato soup. A smidgen of brown sugar and a bit of basil makes it mighty tasty.

1 quart canned tomatoes
1/2 cup chopped celery optional
1/2 cup chopped onion
1 T brown sugar
2 tsp basil
salt to taste (about 1 tsp)

Bring tomatoes, celery and onion to a low boil for 10 minutes. Continue simmering if needed until onion and celery are soft. Remove from heat.

Allow it to cool a bit or easier handling, then puree tomato mixture in the blender. Be careful, it will be hot. Do not let it splash on you. Next, make the soup creamy with a white sauce:

White Sauce:

¼ cup butter
¼ cup flour
½ tsp basil – optional
2 cups milk.

> Tip: Avoid burns when you are blending hot liquids. Lay a dishtowel over the lid of the blender. If any hot soup spurts out from under the lid, the towel will protect your hands and arms

Heat butter in sauce pan until melted. Add 1 cup milk and bring to just below a boil.

Mix flour and the rest of the milk in a shaker container or whisk together thoroughly.

Slowly pour into milk mixture stirring constantly. Simmer until thickened. Stir in basil or any other desired spices.

Stir tomato puree into the white sauce. Heat through and serve.

Goes great with crackers, toast, or (our favorite) grilled cheese sandwiches. Yum!

BLACK BEAN AND HAM SOUP

I discovered this super easy soup quite by accident. Left over black beans and some ham in my refrigerator were lying there waiting to be combined in some delicious way.

I adapted another soup recipe and used what I had. It turned out so well I wrote it down.

Ingredients

- 1 quart chicken broth
- 2 pints canned black beans
- • 1 chopped onion
- 1 clove garlic
- 1 tsp chili powder
- 1 tsp cumin
- 1 tsp salt
- 1 tsp pepper (or to taste)
- 2 cups chopped cooked ham (lunch meat or left over ham from a ham dinner)

Pour chicken broth and black beans into a large pot. Add cumin, salt and pepper. Bring to a boil and keep at a low boil for 10 minutes.

While soup is simmering, sauté onion in a bit of olive oil, or butter. Press or mince garlic and add to the simmering soup.

When onion is tender add to the soup and continue simmering. You could optionally add 1 cup chopped carrots or celery.

Cook until heated through. Cornbread is a great accompaniment to this soup.

CHICKEN AND BLACK BEAN SOUP

Here is another leftover soup that is so easy I had to include it here. First I'll tell you how to make the initial meal.... then how to make soup out of the leftovers.

Day one meal.:2 pints home canned black beans.
4 large boneless, skinless chicken breasts,
1 pint salsa.

Place all this in the crockpot with the salsa poured over the top. Cook on low for 5 to 6 hours. Delicious! Eat dinner and store away leftovers in the fridge.

Next day make your soup:

Remove any chicken leftovers and cut into bite size pieces. Mix back in with your leftover black beans. Add a bit of water if needed. I don't usually have to, but if it is not soupy you may.

Stir, heat and just like that.....you've got a nice chunky black bean and chicken soup.

Carrot Soup

I loved this carrot soup. I must admit my children didn't care for it.... but what do kids know anyway!

2 pounds carrots – peeled
and chopped
1/4 cup butter
2 tsp salt
1 large onion – chopped
2 stalks of celery
2 quarts chicken broth
1/4 tsp white pepper
1/4 cup 1/2 and ½
2 tsp crushed dried dill weed

Sauté chopped carrots and onion in butter. Approximately 10 minutes. Add chicken broth and dill weed. Bring to a boil. Boil 15-20 minutes or until carrots are tender and soft.

Let cool a little and then puree soup in batches until soup is creamy and smooth. Be careful soup is hot... be sure it does not splash out and scald you.

Return creamed soup to the pot and bring back to a simmer. Reduce heat and add cream and pepper. Do not boil after adding cream.

Serve with grilled cheese sandwiches.

Notes: Adding 1/4 tsp cayenne pepper adds a bit of spice - optional.

POTATO CORN CHOWDER

This is traditional potato chowder. I like it with the corn but my husband doesn't care for corn in soups. Leave it in or out as you choose.

Ingredients

¼ pound bacon, cooked crisp and crumbled
1 small onion chopped (about 1 cup)
1 quart tomatoes, drained, Or use 1 can tomato sauce. (12 oz)
½ to 1 pint corn drained (optional)
2 tsp salt
¼ tsp pepper
½ tsp paprika
1 quart chicken broth
4 potatoes diced. (peeled if you prefer)
1 cup milk

Cook bacon until crisp. Cook chopped onion in bacon drippings until soft. Add tomatoes, corn, salt, pepper, paprika, chicken broth.

Bring to a boil and simmer 10 minutes, Add chopped potatoes and continue cooking until potatoes are soft. Add milk. You can use whole milk, cream, or evaporated milk.

Serve with crackers, muffins, corn bread or toast.

TORTILLA SOUP

This tortilla soup is made mild with Anaheim peppers. For soup with a kick, substitute minced jalapeno.

Ingredients:
1 tablespoon vegetable oil
8 / 6-inch corn tortillas, cut into pieces approximately 1 inch.
1 cup chopped onion
1 Anaheim Pepper chopped (I freeze these each year)
1 clove garlic
1 quart home canned tomato sauce
1 tablespoon ground cumin
1 quart home canned chicken broth
2 cups cooked chopped chicken (or substitute pork)
1 tsp salt (or to taste)
cheddar cheese
sour cream

In a large saucepan (a cast iron dutch oven works great) heat oil and saute onion peppers and garlic. Add ½ the tortilla strips and heat for 2 minutes stirring often.

Add the quart of tomatoes. Bring to a boil and simmer for 10 minutes. Stir in the chicken broth and cumin. Simmer uncovered for 40 – 50 minutes. This will thicken the soup.

Turn off the heat and let the soup cool slightly. Place half the soup in a blender and puree until smooth. Return puree to the pot. Stir in the chicken. Heat thoroughly and serve with grated cheddar cheese and sour cream.

Tortilla chips or corn bread go with this very well.

Bacon can be substituted for the ham. Be sure and cook prior to adding it to your soup.

A ham bone can be used as well. Simply add the ham bone when you would add the ham. When you are ready to add your potatoes, remove the ham bone. Pull off any meat and return meat to the soup.

Grandma's Chicken Soup

This Recipe is from Donna Archambault, It looks delicious!
Those Grandmothers usually pass on great recipes don't
they.

14 cups water
1- 15 oz. can chicken broth
1 split chicken breast (bone in, skin on)
4-5 stalks of celery cut in 4-5 inch segments.
1 large onion
1 quart jar of canned stewed tomatoes
1 quart jar of canned carrots (I usually use 1/2 the jar)
6-8 medium boiler type potatoes (peeled and left whole)
2 Tbs spoons dehydrated parsley (you can use fresh)
Salt and pepper to taste.

In a stock pot put water, broth, whole onion, and chicken.
Bring to a boil Skim any fat that appears at the top.

Reduce heat to medium add tomatoes, celery, parsley and continue to simmer about 30 min (adding a little water as needed if too much liquid evaporates.)

Add whole peeled potatoes, bring to a boil reduce heat and add your canned carrots.

Simmer another 30 min. Remove potatoes, carrots, celery and chicken from pot (this will be served as a plated boiled dinner)

Take broth (you can strain it if you like) serve with noodles (we make our own).

My Hungarian grandmother always served this soup with the broth and noodles separate from the meat and vegetables.

Over the years my Mom made a few changes and so have I. It is a good basic recipe that you can add what you want according to your likes.

CHEESY BROCCOLI SOUP

If you like broccoli you will love this cheesy creamy broccoli soup. Creamy and tasty.

3 cups dried broccoli, re-hydrated to 2 1/2 to 3 cups.
1/4 cup freeze dried onion
1 quart chicken broth.
1 T flour
1/4 tsp garlic powder or 1
clove garlic.
1 1/2 tsp salt
dash of black pepper
2 cups milk
1 heaping cup cubed cheddar cheese - this should be around 1/4 to 1/2 pound.

Combine re-hydrated broccoli, onion, and chicken broth. Bring to a boil and simmer until veggies are soft. A minimum of 10 minutes.

Let cool slightly and remove 1/2 of the vegetable mixture to a blender. Blend until smooth. Return to soup pot. I like this soup chunky so that is all I do. You could go ahead and make a smooth soup by blending all of it.

Add the flour, garlic powder, salt and pepper. Stir and reheat.

Slowly add the milk and cheese. Cook on low stirring constantly until cheese is melted.

Do not boil. If you boil this the milk products will separate and give it a funny texture. It still tastes good but much nicer if it is smooth and creamy with chunks of broccoli.

Serve with bread, crackers or cornbread.

You could add 2 cups cooked rice to this as well to make it go farther for a crowd. Or if your meal simply has to have meat. Add some chopped cooked ham at the end.

Tequila Chili

This recipe is from Morgan Rayl. Tequila Chili, that'll warm your insides!

One qt. ground beef (you can substitute any meat you want, we do turkey often)
One qt stewed tomatoes or any canned tomatoes (pictured with Sun Burst tomatoes)
One small can tomato paste
One or two cans chili beans (depend on if you like lots of beans or little beans)
Small onion chopped (optional)
One or two clove garlic minced
one pint canned corn, drained
2oz tequila (optional)

Put the meat, onion and garlic in a soup pot, cook till onions are soft. Stir often. Add remaining ingredients. Simmer for 10min, stirring often. Then its ready to serve. If you put the tequila you may want to cook for a little extra longer to make sure all the alcohol has cooked off.

Top with grated cheese, onions, sour cream, and/or chives and serve with corn bread or crackers!

The original recipe was from my mother-in-law. I tried to make chili several times when my husband and I were 1st married but my husband was never a fan of it.He kept saying it's not moms.

So one time when we were visiting her I asked her to show me how to make it.

After I started canning I modified it to use the ingredients from my canning collection. We love to eat it on cold days. I look forward all summer to make it!

Portuguese Bean and Cabbage Soup

I adapted this soup from a recipe I found in my power company monthly newsletter. Sometimes these are the best places to find recipes!

I adapted the ingredients to using home canned and dehydrated foods.

Ingredients

1 pound sausage of your choice. Spicy or not.
½ cup dehydrated carrots
2 potatoes diced
1 small onion chopped
2 quarts home canned tomatoes
1 T salt
1T honey
1 T dried peppers. Try dried Anaheim peppers... or use something spicier to make it lively!

Brown the sausage. I used a ground venison sausage. If you are using a link type sausage slice and brown. Add the rest of the above ingredients. Simmer 40 minutes.

Then add:

1 quart home canned pinto beans. (other beans would probably work too)

1 large head of cabbage sliced thin. (about a 2 pound head)

1 ½ quarts water – this is an estimate. Sometimes I'll need to add more or less.

Simmer this another 20 – 30 minutes or until veggies are tender. Serve with homemade bread to soak up the last drop!

CROCK POT SPLIT PEA SOUP

Split pea soup is another favorite to make with a leftover ham bone.

Ingredients:

1 (16 oz.) pkg. dried green split peas, rinsed
1 ham bone - I save the bone from a ham dinner or you could use chopped leftover ham.
½ cup dried carrots
1 onion chopped

1/4 cup dried zucchini
2 stalks celery chopped
1 clove of garlic, minced or crushed
1 tbsp. salt (or to taste)
1/2 tsp. fresh pepper
2 qt chicken broth

Place all ingredients in slow cooker.

Cover and cook on HIGH 4 to 5 hours or on low 8 to 10 hours until peas are very soft and ham falls off bone.

Remove ham bone and cut off leftover meat. Return to the soup. Stir vigorously to smash up peas and serve.

Perfect with cornbread.

Northern Bean Soup

I love to make a bean soup with leftover ham and mashed potatoes. Makes a whole new meal out of the leftovers.

Ingredients

2 cups dry Northern Beans
8 cups water
1 quart canned tomatoes
1 quart chicken broth
2 cups chopped ham
1 large onion chopped(or

¼ cup dried)
1 tsp salt – or to taste
½ tsp pepper
1 clove garlic – crushed.
2 cups mashed potatoes
1 cup dried carrots
½ cup dried zucchini

Prepare:

Heat water and beans to boiling, boil 2 minutes. Remove from heat, cover and let stand for 1 hour. Drain. Add tomatoes, ham, onion, carrots, zucchini, salt, pepper and garlic to the beans. Heat to boiling. Reduce heat and simmer for 10 minutes.

Place soup in a crock pot and turn on low. Cook 5 to 6 hours. Check occasionally and add water if needed. Add mashed potatoes and stir gently to blend and thicken about 1 hour prior to eating.

Notes:

½ cup or so of cream or half and half can be added to this if desired.

ACORN SQUASH SOUP

I created this soup from leftover acorn squash for my lunch one afternoon. I am the only one in this family who loves acorn soup.... so this makes a small batch. It was just enough for 2 bowls. Double or triple as needed.

Ingredients:

about 3/4 cup cooked acorn squash.
1 pint chicken broth
1/2 to 1 tsp salt -according to your taste.
shake of pepper
1/2 cup evaporated milk. (you could also use 1/2 and 1/2 or other cream)
pinch of garlic powder- I used a 1/8 measuring tsp but did not fill the spoon level.

Directions:

Scoop out your squash from the rind if needed. Combine squash with 1 pint chicken broth, salt, pepper and garlic powder. Simmer 15 minutes. Stir occasionally breaking up the squash.

Add 1/2 cup evaporated milk. Stir and heat. Serve with bread or crackers of your choice.

Dried Veggie and Potato Soup

Potato soup made with home canned potatoes and dried veggies.

2 pints canned potatoes
1 pint chicken broth
1 pound bacon
1/3 cup dried carrots
1/3 cup dried zucchini
1 onion
2 tsp salt
pepper

Fry bacon until crispy. Remove from pan and set aside. Saute onion in the remaining bacon grease until clear and soft.

Add to your soup pot, 1 pint chicken broth, 2 pints canned potatoes and onion. Bring to a boil, reduce heat and simmer for 10 minutes.

Allow soup to cool slightly, then puree in a blender in batches until it is smooth and creamy. OR if you like chunky potato soup just use a potato masher and mash up the biggest chunks of potatoes leaving some smaller "chunks".

Return to your soup pot and add dried veggies, bacon, salt and pepper. Simmer until veggies are re-hydrated and done. Be sure and stir often.

If he soup starts getting too thick simply add a bit of water to keep it soupy. Serve!

Note: Adding the dried veggies is optional.

Ham can be substituted for the bacon.

If you want you can put this in the crock pot to cook the dried veggies.

Simply place in the crock after pureeing or mashing. Add your veggies and meat. Cook for 4-5 hours or until the dried veggies are rehydrated and done.

SOPA

If you've got a cold try this soup by Marilyn.

"My X father in law from Mexico City used to make this soup. It is wonderful for a bad cold with a stuffy nose.

All ingredients are by taste you really can't go wrong, I've never actually measured but this should be close."

1 14.5 oz can of tomatoes chopped
2 slices of bacon chopped cooked but not till crisp
1/2 an onion chopped
1 clove garlic chopped
1 1/2 cup of chopped cabbage (somewhat large pieces)
1 Jalapeno seeded and chopped (I use 2)
1 to 1 1/2 cup of beef broth.

Throw it all in a pan and let simmer for an hour or so.

Pumpkin Soup

1 onion chopped small
4 cups pumpkin pulp
1 quart and 1 pint chicken broth
¼ tsp dried parsley
pinch of thyme
1 garlic clove pressed
½ cup half and half or other cream

Stir all this together and simmer for 30 minutes or so. You can eat it as is, or if you'd like a smooth soup blend it in a blender in batches. Again use caution, it will be hot.

Love this with saltine crackers and slices of sharp cheddar cheese.

TACO SOUP

Even my finicky eaters love this soup.

1 pound beef, venison or elk cubed
2 cups water
2 cubes beef bouillon
¼ cup dried carrots
¼ cup dried zucchini (optional)
2 T dried minced onion
1 T taco seasoning

1 T dry ranch dressing mix
1 quart canned tomato
½ pint salsa
2 pints canned black beans
½ cup sliced black olives (optional)
1T honey

Brown venison in a pressure cooker, then add 2 cups water, 2 bouillon cubes and the dried vegetables. Bring to 10 pounds pressure and maintain for 10 minutes.

Remove from heat and cool quickly by running cold water over the cooker.

Add canned tomatoes , salsa, taco seasoning, ranch dressing mix, black beans, olives and honey. Mix well, heat through. Serve with a dollop of sour cream, tortilla chips, or

Quesadillas

Quesadilla – (fancy term for cheesy tortillas) Place a flour tortilla on a hot frying pan and sprinkle some cheese over it. Add another tortilla on top. Cover. Heat until cheese is melted. Flipping once. Slice into wedges and serve with your soup.

Notes: If you don't have a pressure cooker you can still make this soup. Simply follow the same instructions except you will need a longer cook time for your dried veggies. Just simmer until done.

CHICKEN BARLEY SOUP

I love tossing stuff in the crock pot and having a meal come
out of it all

Ingredients

1 Quart home canned chicken legs - bone in.
3 quarts water
1/3 cup dehydrated carrots
1/3 cup dehydrated onion
1/3 cup dehydrated zucchini
1/4 cup lentils
1/4 cup barley
2 garlic cloves - or more to taste
1 tsp dill weed
1 Tbs salt - to taste
1/4 tsp pepper - to taste

Prepare

The first thing you'll need to do is to pull out any bones from your canned chicken. If you've canned the chicken boneless then obviously you won't need this step. Don't drain the liquid just separate the bones.

Then add 1 quart water to your chicken and bring to a boil. Simmer for 10 minutes. In the meantime add the rest of the ingredients to the crock pot.

When the chicken is done simmering add it to the crock and give it a stir.

Cook on low for 5 to 6 hours. As this cooks check on it every once in a while. The dehydrated foods soak up water and you may need more. Just keep it soupy!

Serve with the usual soup sides, bread, cheese, crackers.

CANNING SOUP AND BROTH

Safe canning practices for adapting any soup recipe for canning and storage on the shelf

Importance of Correct Processing

Canning Broth or Stock MUST be done with a pressure canner. There is no way around this. Processing in a boiling water bath for many hours is not a substitute for the pressure canner!

With any low acid food there is the risk of botulism. Botulism is a serious food poisoning that at its worst can be fatal. You don't want to mess around with it.

So how do we get rid of it??? Heat. Botulism can be prevented by processing at temperatures above 240 degrees F. This is only achievable in a pressure canner.

A long waterbath is no substitute for the pressure canner. No matter how long you waterbath something you won't reach that temperature.

I've included step by step instructions for canning broth or stock. I've also included directions for canning your own homemade soup recipe.

If you have not canned broth or soup before, I recommend that you read these instructions through to the end before you start. If you have not used your pressure canner before, read the instruction booklet that came with the canner.

ALTITUDE ADJUSTMENTS

I'll say it again! Proper processing is very important.

As your altitude goes above 1000 feet above sea level the atmospheric pressure is reduced. This causes water to boil at lower temperatures. A pressure canner must reach a temperature of 240 degrees Fahrenheit.

To compensate at higher altitudes you must increase the amount of pressure used. The time does not change, only the pressure used.

Altitude Adjustments for Pressure Canner		
Altitude in Feet	Dial Gauge Canner	Weighted Gauge Canner
0-1000	10	10
1001-2000	11	15
2001-4000	12	15
4001-6000	13	15
6001-8000	14	15
8000-10,000	15	15

If you are above 1000 feet elevation use this chart to determine your correct pressure. This chart applies to all three canning methods found in this book.

HOMEMADE STOCK OR BROTH

What's the difference between Homemade Broth or Stock? Many people (myself included) use the terms stock and broth interchangeably. My understanding of the differences:

• Homemade Stock is made from the bones or less meaty parts. The neck, back, and wings of chicken are examples. Or use the carcass from a roast chicken meal. This turns out to be a darker richer color and flavor.

• Homemade Broth is made from meatier pieces with the meat on. The meat is cooked and removed (save it for casseroles etc.) and the bones further cooked. It has a lighter color and flavor.

Here I show chicken stock made with more bones and veggies in the darker jars on the left. The lighter color jars on the right are chicken broth made with meatier pieces and without veggies.

FIRST MAKE YOUR HOMEMADE BROTH

I've used chicken in these instructions since that is what I make 90% of the time. The same basic steps are followed if you want to make beef broth as well. You'd just substitute beef bones and meat.

Gather your supplies
• large stock pot or pressure canner
• bowls
• large spoons
• sharp knife
• towels and dish cloths

Ingredients

Chicken pieces. Any chicken parts will do. I prefer to skin my pieces but again it is not necessary. Approximately 6 pounds (this is with meat on, if you have bones you won't need as much) will be enough for a batch in my large stock pot. I usually get at least 7 quarts out of this.

Quick Tip: Save left over bones or carcass, and vegetables in your freezer until you have enough to make your broth or stock.

If you want to make a beef broth use beef soup bones. These can often be purchased in the meat section of a grocery store. You can also save the bones from roasts.

Vegetables and seasonings are optional. This could include 2-3 Stalks of celery - chopped in large chunks. 2 onions - quartered, 2-3 Carrots - chopped in large chunks.

Place bones or chicken pieces in your stock pot. Fill with water. Bring to a boil.

Add vegetables and seasonings if you are going to use them. Simmer until meat is done. About 1 hour.

Use a slotted spoon or tongs to remove chicken pieces. Let the chicken pieces cool until you can handle it well enough to remove the meat. Remove the meat from the bones and save for other uses. Great for chicken enchiladas, chicken casseroles etc.

Cut or break any large bones into shorter pieces. Be careful not to burn yourself. Return the bones to the stock pot.

Don't be too fanatical about this step. If you are handling a thigh bone that won't easily break it is not a big deal. Just toss it back into the pot. The purpose is to allow the water more access to the nutritious marrow in the bones.

Next you have 2 options to cook the carcass and bones.

• Option one: Simmer low for several hours. The more you simmer the better. 6-8 hours.

• Option two (my preference): Use a pressure canner and cook at 10 pounds pressure for 1 hour. Allow canner to release pressure and continue recipe. This saves a lot of time and brings out more of the nutrition from the bones.

Remove bones and vegetables. Discard. Strain broth to remove any small bones and pieces left in the broth. I have a colander that I use. You can use cheesecloth if you want a very clear broth. I don't mind little bits of meat so the colander is good for me.

Many people who are cutting back on fat will allow the broth to cool and remove the fat. I don't bother with this step... but it is an option.

Allow the broth to cool, and then place in the fridge to cool completely. The next morning there will be a layer of fat floating on top. It is easy then to remove that fat with a slotted spoon then store your broth.

 Now you have a nice nutritious broth for use in recipes. This can be frozen or canned.

Canning Your Prepared Broth

Gather your supplies

• pressure canner
• canning jars
• canning seals and rings
• jar lifter
• canning funnel
• chicken broth

Start by preparing jars and get water in your canner heating. Place jars and lids in simmering hot water to warm and keep warm.

Bring broth to a boil and pour hot broth into hot jars. Wipe the rims of your jars clean and place on your lid and rings. Leave 1 inch head space.

Process - Always adjust for your altitude.

pints - process for 20 minutes, quarts - process for 25 minutes

When processing time is done let your canner come back to zero pressure naturally. Do not try to speed up the process by pouring cool water over the canner or any other method. Just leave the canner alone to cool.

Once canner has released all pressure, open the canner and let some steam out. Leave the lid set on the pot. Let jars sit in the canner for 5 minutes. This allows jars to cool slowly and reduces siphoning. (When liquid is lost due to uneven pressure)

Carefully remove jars to a counter and allow to cool overnight. When completely cool check the seals. If any jars did not seal they may be stored in the fridge and used within a few days. Wash your jars if needed and remove the rings.

Store your jars in a cool dark environment. Usually a pantry is fine.

Congratulations! You now have healthy homemade broth to use in soups, stews, chili and more. And the best part is..... you know exactly what is in that jar!

DIRECTIONS FOR CANNING YOUR HOMEMADE SOUP

Home canning soup is a wonderful way to have quick lunches ready. There are a few things to remember.

Soups will always need to be pressure canned.

Do not add noodles, rice, flour, cream or any milk or any thickeners. All these can be added when you heat the soup to serve it.

If you are using beans or peas they must be cooked prior to canning.

It is also not recommended to can pureed type soups.... I do not give directions for this. However, what I would do to solve this problem..... Just can it chunky. Then when you open the jar to serve it, puree it at that point.

Directions

First cook any meats and vegetables. If you are using beans cook them by covering dried beans with water by a couple of inches. Bring to a boil and simmer for 2 minutes, remove from the heat cover and let soak for at least 1 hour and drain.

Combine all solid ingredients and add whatever broth you may be using. Chicken broth, beef broth, canned tomatoes or water. Add spices and seasoning at this point as well.

Bring to a boil and simmer for 5 minutes. Remember no dairy, thickeners, pasta or rice. These can be added later when you serve the soup.

Fill your jars leaving a 1 inch head space. Be sure to fill each jar about halfway full with the solid ingredients. I use a slotted spoon. Then add the liquid to the cover.

This way you don't end up with some jars being mostly broth and others having too many solid ingredients.

There is also a safety reason for using half solids and half liquid. You want the heat to penetrate fully to the center of the jar. If your soup is too thick, it may not do so. Using enough liquid can also be helpful if you'll be adding noodles or ice when you serve it.

When your jars are full you will process them in a pressure canner. Do NOT process in a waterbath canner

If you need more instruction on how to run a pressure canner, see your canner's manual. Or you can go to Simply Canning .com/pressure canning

Process pints 60 minutes, quarts 75 minutes. Be sure to use the correct pressure according to your elevation. If your soup has seafood you will need process either pints or quarts for 100 minutes.

Adjustments for Pressure Canner

Altitude in Feet	Dial Gauge Canner	Weighted Gauge Canner
0-1000	10	10
1001-2000	11	15
2001-4000	12	15
4001-6000	13	15

BREADS

Because homemade bread makes ANY soup better!

WHOLE WHEAT BREAD RECIPE

This whole wheat bread recipe is the recipe I use for our daily bread. Easy and forgiving even for a beginner. As with all my whole wheat recipes I use hard white wheat for the best results.

Ingredients
1 cup warm water
1 egg
1/3 cup sugar
1 tsp salt
1 T Vital Wheat Gluten
3 1/3 cups whole wheat flour
2 T butter
1 T active dry yeast

Add warm water, egg, sugar, salt, gluten, and flour to your bread machine. Water should not be hot enough to burn your hands. Between 110- 120 degrees is perfect. I know that my hot tap water is just about right. If you are not sure check the temperature the first couple of times with a thermometer.

Cut butter into 4 pieces and place one in each corner of your machine. Make a little well in the middle of your dry ingredients, add yeast to this well.

Set your machine on dough and run the cycle. I check my dough after about 5 minutes of kneading. If the dough seems to dry or wet add a tablespoon of water or flour accordingly.

Knowing the correct feel of bread dough is something comes with practice. When I first started making bread I almost always made my dough too dry. I'd suggest erring on the wet side.... but not too sticky. Usually the measurements I list with this recipe work just about right. But when making bread even the humidity of the day will have an effect on your dough.

When the machine is done, remove your dough to a lightly floured surface. Knead a 5 - 10 times. Form into a smooth loaf and place in an oiled bread pan. Let rise in a warm place about 10 - 15 minutes.

This time will vary. The dough will approximately double. It should just reach the top of the bread pan. Remember the dough will raise more as it bakes. Don't let it rise too much or your bread will be too airy and crumbly.

I let my dough rise right in the oven. I have a gas stove and it works well for me to turn on the oven just until I hear the pilot turn on to throw some heat in and then turn it off. Leave the door closed and the oven will stay warm and the bread will rise nicely.

When the dough has risen turn the oven on 350 and bake until a nice golden brown. This will take about 20 minutes.

Notes:

I usually make one loaf in my bread machine and then make another batch in my kitchen aide mixer with the bread hook at the same time. Add the ingredients in the same manner as the bread machine.

I keep an eye on them and coordinate my mixer with the machine.

The bread machine is programmed to knead for a specific length of time and rest the dough for a length of time. I simply take my cue from it and run the mixer at the same times. Then I can bake both loaves at the same time.

CAST IRON CORN BREAD

1 cup cornmeal
1 cup whole wheat flour
½ tsp salt
4 tsp baking powder
1 T sugar (or honey)
1 egg
1 cup milk
¼ cup butter

Preheat your oven to 425 degrees. Mix cornmeal, flour, salt and baking powder together in a bowl.

Add your egg, milk and softened butter.

Mix well.

Pour in a greased heavy pan approximately 8 inches square. I love to use my cast iron frying pan. It makes a beautiful browned crust on the bottom.

Bake at 425 degrees for 20 – 25 minutes.

Serve with lots of butter or honey.

Whole Wheat Focaccia Bread

An Italian Flat bread recipe flavored with Parmesan cheese, garlic salt and rosemary. Great with homemade soup.

Ingredients

3/4 cup +3 T water
3 cups whole wheat flour
2 T dry milk
3 1/2 T sugar
1 tsp salt
3 T butter
2 tsp active dry yeast
2 T olive oil
2 T grated Parmesan cheese
2 tsp rosemary
1 tsp garlic salt (or to taste)

Add water, flour, dry milk, sugar and salt to bread machine. Cut butter into 4 pieces and add to corners of bread machine. Make a well in the center of dry ingredients and add yeast.

Run machine on dough cycle. When done remove dough to a lightly floured surface and knead for 1 minute.

Roll dough out to fit a cookie sheet. About 15x10 inches. I use my stoneware bar pan.

Cover and let rise for 20 minutes or until risen slightly. Make an indentation every few inches with the handle of a wooden spoon.

Brush dough with olive oil. Sprinkle on Parmesan cheese, rosemary leaves and garlic salt.

Bake at 400 degrees for 15 minutes or until lightly browned. Cut into squares to serve.   This goes great with any soup.

Whole Wheat Dinner Roll Recipe

The ingredients for this dinner roll recipe are the same as the recipe I use for our daily bread. It works great for a dinner roll recipe as well. Add the suggested herbs and you've got great herbed dinner rolls for a special dinner.

Ingredients

1 cup hot water
1 egg
1/3 cup sugar
1 tsp salt
2 T butter
1 T Vital Wheat Gluten
3 1/3 cups whole wheat flour
1 T active dry yeast
1/2 tsp each Oregano, Basil, Thyme, Rosemary

I make the dough for these dinner rolls in my bread machine and then shape my rolls and bake.

First add warm water, egg, sugar, salt, gluten, and flour to your bread machine. Add herbs to this mix if you want an herbed roll, or leave out for regular whole wheat rolls.

Cut butter into 4 pieces and place one in each corner of your machine. Make a little well in the middle of your dry ingredients, add yeast to this well.

Set your machine on dough and run the cycle. I check my dough after about 5 minutes of kneading. If the dough seems to dry or wet add a tablespoon of water or flour accordingly.

When the machine is done, remove your dough to a lightly floured surface. Knead a 5 - 10 times. Divide into 4 equal pieces

Divide those 4 sections into 2 equal pieces each. The final sections divide into thirds. You should end up with 12 small pieces of dough.

Arrange in a square pan so the pieces are just barley touching. Let rise in a warm place about 10 minutes. I let mine rise in my oven.

This time will vary. The pieces will touch each other more but not overly crowded. Remember the dough will rise more as it bakes.

I use my oven to keep the dough warm while it rises. My gas stove works well if I turn it on just until I hear the pilot light turn on then turn the temperature off.

If you have an electric oven turn it on just enough to throw some heat in and warm it up a bit. Then turn it off. Keep the door shut and it keeps warm for the dough to rise.

When the dough has risen turn the oven on 350 and bake until a nice golden brown. This will take about 20 minutes.

Slather with butter and enjoy!

Also Available

Simple Steps Canning Guide

Canning Safety for the Complete Beginner.

Understand the process of canning and how it preserves your food.

Elk and Venison Recipes

How to Can It..... How to Use It.

From the Field to the Table, It's all in YOUR hands. Doesn't it feel good! Learn how to preserve the results of your hard hunting. Then try some great recipes using it.

Visit SimplyCanning.com for either of these titles.